T0161966

RISE

UP

RISE

WAVE BOOKS   SEATTLE   NEW YORK

MATTHEW ROHRER

Published by Wave Books

www.wavepoetry.com

Copyright © 2007 by Matthew Rohrer

Wave Books titles are distributed to the trade by
Consortium Book Sales and Distribution
1045 Westgate Drive, St. Paul, Minnesota 55114

Library of Congress Cataloging-in-Publication Data
Rohrer, Matthew.
Rise up / Matthew Rohrer. — 1st ed.
p. cm.
ISBN 13: 978-1-933517-19-3
[LIMITED EDITION HARDCOVER]
ISBN 13: 978-1-933517-18-6
[TRADE PAPER]
I. Title.
PS3568.052R57 2007
811´.54—dc22
2006038909

Designed and composed by Quemadura
Printed in the United States of America

9 8 7 6 5 4 3 2 1

FIRST EDITION

Wave Books 009

δικέμον

[MINE]

CONTENTS

To be rigid and arrogant;

to be above this generation and distant from its ways;

to talk of great principles;

to be critical and disparaging;

these are approved by scholars who dwell in the mountains,

by men who are not of this age . . .

CHUANG TZU

FOUR ROMANTIC POETS

1

I am emotionally translucent.
I am on the new sofa. I am wedged
between the 2 walls of the stoop. I am
unwashed & I'm self-conscious about it.
I am not helping. I make her feel like
she's eaten a spoonful of peanut butter.
And now she's slid back into a green sleep
in early Autumn and she will escape
out the back. If only the universe
weren't shaped so much like me, I might change
my approach. I must learn to say what I
never intended to say, like John Clare.
The good news is I saw the open door
of a gentle wonder, where I want to live.

The repetitive poems of the Book
of Songs, the blazing peach blossoms falling
in every stanza, and on the winding
path through the shade to the wedding: teach me
to hold an image of the world in me
that isn't cracked, that isn't bent backwards
like my toenail, catching on the bedspread.
In you is the end of feeling vanquished
by the bloodthirsty administration
of bright, brittle laws. Underneath your stalks
of millet old soldiers' bones are moaning
out to me: reap not! turn yourself away
from the brightly-lit path, & take a side
path beneath the shadowy pines, & stop.

Outside the Picnic House, outside the wedding
full of wine but still greedy for it inside
my suit, the black trees along the parkway
blacken further when the storm flashes behind
them. I wait on a damp dark wood chip path
for companions. There is music
everywhere in the trees & a DJ places
all of life's emphasis in my black rubber
heels, and my sleeveless wife is a serpent
unearthed in the lightning: pale & fast.
I pop 5 chocolates in my mouth & chew.

Perpetual Halloween.

The Aztec people.

Horror & death.

A man walking down the street.

A man looking intently at a woman.

And running into a fire hydrant.

And crumpling.

The absolute rightness of it.

The love between all people.

The covenant.

A crowd under the eaves on an autumn night.

Wet leaves and feet.

The poems of Shelley.

The love between all people.

Sitting by the window in the flashing storm.

Sitting at the window certain of this.

The connection between people in a room.

The vow that penetrates space.

The cold light of stars.

SUMMER POEM

The port town of Koper is hot,
the hills and vineyards of Brda are hot,
Park Slope is miserable, somewhere a storm
waits for us, it scoots. Sunset Park is hot,
Greenwood Heights is an imaginary place
that is stifling, the sound of a banjo in this heat
is grand. Men gallop in sombreros
in Bolivia, porcupine sabers
shake and torment the tree of life.
The steaming green tree.
The curling, burning edges of the love poem
in Chile. It is unbearable in Chile.
Piscataway is uninhabitable.
Crown Heights is sluggish.
The museum is closed, the 2nd floor is melting.
No one is happy
but the rich, who are very happy.

WINNING ISN'T EVERYTHING

1

You can't do this to me, cry
us both to sleep at the end
of summer. Your sister said
autumn is sad, winter hurts,
but people who say things are
always wrong. There's a touch of
madness in the air, New York
is friendly. Money burrows
its way to the very core
of the Earth. It's time for us
to leave the Earth

2

Labor Day weekend is a free
day that's overcast and dark.
A tinny radio from
a backyard, a grey stillness.
I'm hallucinating cries
again, I don't move, I don't
hear anything. I've failed.
I love nonsense and hatred.
A jungle or a desert
will overtake me.

"I'm frightened and too lazy
to think things through, I'm going
to vote with my ass. I am
casting my vote for dumb luck
and vengeance." Put the paper
down and walk along the beach.
Mute, beautiful clouds build up
in a blue space that is too
towering to maim. Patience
is interchangeable with the sand.
Winning isn't everything.

THIS POSTCARD

this
bucolic postcard
reaches out to strangers
marvelous to number
a soft air that falls across
mirth & dread is
darkness, is my mistress
I feel lighter, I am going on her trip
I rise, rise through
the eternal day
but she cannot hear me, she does not live
solely in my mind
when the sky seems holy
mysterious
lead me out of my own heart
but lock her heart
quiet birches rise up

POEM IN THE MANNER OF COLERIDGE

Of that house—that was more like frigid rooms
in a dingy, linoleum-tiled hive
and was home to manic ex-cons
—let us not banish that feeling, there, that we were
a miniature Earth, beset on all sides
by waves of dangerous subatomic
particles of other people's unease.
All things pierced by neutrinos but intact,
and our planetary defense was sound.
Let us recall the corner bagel place
with pleasure as a spot to occupy
the infant & me when a nor'easter
drove us away from the splintery gym.
Let us drink to the collapse of real estate.

POEM AGAINST WORDSWORTH

The robin chasing the butterfly
marvelous and fierce
and the butterfly fleeing
the bird is powdered bright
with beauty
and the robin ceases
its pursuit to cock its head
at laughter

the butterfly has terrible
powers of insinuation
It cannot be trusted
It alights, in delight
like an agate
you will never speak to it
The robin's eye
is a hole opening
into a universe
which is contemplating a river

Waves and particles of light
bring peace to me
beside the water
but are not peace
a butterfly deliberate and slow
drowning
a robin in a black cat's dream
speaking in the street
of the crushing will to live

POEM [DESCRIBE THE SHAPE]

Describe the shape
of an enormous L to do
the laundry on Monday morning.
The day is open and blue and no
one else is alive.
My wife was crawling on
the floor last night.
A few lights burning across the way.
A swoosh sweeps it
all away this morning.
And it is carted away through
the open windows. Grackles
man the spires in the sky.
Bring blue milk home from
the corner where they
bottle the day.

POEM ON THE RADIO

The radio said rain in the evening
and being trusting & full of life
I led us to a shady hill & the rain
drew inwards to the earth in long white lines.
I kneeled beneath a tree, mysterious
light welled up from the mud. Somewhere the birds
took themselves away—to the gray harbor?
Someone bottle this and send it to them
in the desert, in their brown trucks.

POEM FOR THE EAST RIVER

Slightly cleaner (now) waters of the East
River—I will never plunge into you
though you took Spaulding Gray from us & all
those others, you should have just refused them.
I was going to throw myself in front
of the F train, in dreamworld, but not here.
I think I hear one of Keats' short poems.
And the day is cloudless, as you are
not. A woman approaches me with word
of Jesus on a park bench. Do I look
interested in Jesus? She smiled
at me, which hurt. I came here to be
refreshed, that's why I walked across your back.

POEM GLOWING BLUE AND ORANGE

The tall delphinium is the blue roof
of Akureyri, in the rain flowers
glowing blue & orange, it's not really rain,
a cloud moves through us, the fjord reaches up
with a cloud, the sun does not want me dead.
The small boats rising in the water want
us to see them, see that they're not looking.
Too small. Even in August the threat of
immense frigidity. I put my arm
low around her warm ass, I remember.

A HAWK IS ON HER HEART

A hawk is on her heart. I am going on.
Thirty leagues with a stranger
in the pink sunset. From up here a soft
but an almost cinnabar feel. The mountain
jacks that lock that falls across my face.
The lighter reaches out to the paper,
birches rise in place.
I circle & circle, almost great.

SHARP

Music all day on the stereo. And the rain
in the streets, it's like I'm with friends.
It is hard not to pour a glass of wine in the morning.
I am raining. A red-tailed hawk settles
on an old antenna behind the house
and looks right into my eyes
while I'm on the phone with Ellen. Ellen
I say slowly, I'm sure you will succeed
in your endeavors. Those are
not the words I planned to say.
I was still awakening from a dream of the distant war.

POEM

You called, you're on the train, on Sunday,
I have just taken a shower and await
you. Clouds are slipping in off the ocean,
but the room is gently lit by the green
shirt you gave me. I have been practicing
a new way to say hello and it is fantastic.
You were so sad: goodbye: I was so sad.
All the shops were closed but the sky
was high and blue. I tried to walk it off
but I must have walked in the wrong direction.

IN A BOWER OF ROSEMARY

I hate the people who barely
move, who smack the table
with the flat of the Sword
of the Absolute.
I like to lie on my back & listen
to the tiny chiming of
the sword dissolving in the river.

I want no one to have reason
to hate me, though I hate
them, I hate them all. I lie
on my back
and suck in the clouds
through a long straw

———————

In the president's dream I am
washing other people's laundry
and have to stop and wipe
my hands on my pants
and straighten my hair when

he comes to the workroom to be magnanimous.
I wipe my hands. I do not kill him.
Even in his own dream I do not shake his hand.
"Our lords have wine
and things in plenty because they are blessed."
That is why I made this song.

———

Slightly more imagined
than real: seagulls turning
in thick-falling snow.
And the snow benights the sleeping
pin oak, it dreams, it dreams,
beneath the cobblestones

———

The worst thing would be
to be condemned with a group
of others to be executed
and not to be executed last.

———

Enormous flakes that seem
orange in the yellow sky.
The sky remains yellow through
the night. A big man in a brown coat
shovels the walk
to the Historical House,
where no one goes.
In the kitchen the radio says
it has miles to go before it sleeps.
It is running a small and hopeless campaign
for the presidency.

———

The frost outlives its welcome
in one day. The beautiful motion
beneath the sodium lights,
now you can see the white wind.
Now we're frozen fast.
I drink coffee til I taste the grounds.

I wash the dishes. I entertain
the boy. I crawl towards him
like a spectre. I try to write
a poem when he isn't looking.
I write SUGARAPPLE

THE IDEOGRAMS

Five days later I thought
of a good comeback.
I want to come back to the still gloomy sea.
Any deviation from the plan makes me crazy.
The rain fell all over Minnesota's beer halls.
The streets were wet and confusing.
You were sleeping at home
in the cat-blackened gloom.
I'll be home in four days.
I have new shoes,
sunny music.
The sun is shining.
The sun is shining on the river.
But I am like the rain
falling on an abandoned couch
with a tree growing out of the middle of it.
You are the tree.

I hear my baby crying.

Even when he's not crying.

I hear steamships.

I hear phantoms.

The baby is not crying anymore.

All of my love rushes outwards to fill

the empty city. Rush. Rushes out of my ears.

Do you hear that? she says.

It sounds like a boxer punching a horse

through the top half of a barn door.

I am all alone, writing this on a swing.

I can't stop looking up.

It kills the mind.

A cloud looks like a pig and a rat embracing.

They're breaking up.

I wonder if you can see it.

I wonder how much you miss me.

At night I make a little sound.

It sounds like a witch opening a birthday present.

I enjoy trembling with you on the carpet.
But then the poem recedes into the night.
And my fingers recede into your dream.
A photograph of your face has power,
power that fills the room at night,
blue power that fills the room with blue snow.
I startle awake, my fingers still flutter in your dream
and I am startled by the appearance of a lithe witch in the snow.

Use shoes as a pillow beside the lake,
and sleep, sleep, beneath the airplanes sleep
on the moist grass, until the clouds become criminal.
You have suffered armored wings for twenty years.
Eating and dancing like an orangutan, you are mired
in the crops. In your pathetic armor
you are like a fat man fallen partway through the floor
while watching TV.
Passion! Passion! You can unfurl your passion.
You can pretend to have serious phantoms.

Where are you, what are you doing
while we stoke the everlasting campfire?
Hundreds of particular plants and flowers
are calling your name.
The butterflies of love descend to the creek's deformed campaign.
In the city you discuss parlor romances
and novels about torture chambers.
A ballet dancer with a poorly-concealed erection
twirls beneath a light.
Where on all the peaks around this blue valley
will we find you?

Bank the coals against the anguishes of night.
In the afternoon the mountain laurel is awake.
It wakes me up.
The wild mountain orchid droops on the path.
We march and descend.
The men at the campfire pretend to color the rain clouds.
At night this is what scares me:
Having to piss in the forest blackness:
Seeing a faint glow:
Knowing it is two elk working together
to balance a birthday cake on their antlers.

I almost understand you.
Then I come upon you as upon a tree
bristling with spent arrows.
I've come too late.
You kiss me goodbye sometimes
and I feel you transfer everything.
Sometimes you destroy crystal snowballs.
Sometimes I call you three times in one hour.
The pond that separates us during the day is being drained.
You kiss my hand and I see the folly in my plan.
Let the products sell themselves.

The train drew my family
through Rijeka steaming to the embarkation.
To the Adriatic Sea.
If you pause long enough the 500 steps of the pilgrimage
will kneel down to you,
the highest point in Rijeka.
The church where my ancestors saw two invisible Spaniards
riding small donkeys.
Rijeka was steaming.
They went to find an umbrella outside a café.
They never wrote a word of criticism.
A big ship with monstrous screws waited for them
in a sea of beer.

You leave the apartment.
You bring home the bacon.
Once you walked all the way home eating
jalapeños from a jar.
All day I think about words
and how words can topple and humiliate my enemies.
I walk for hours this way with my son
in a small carriage through the humid beech trees.
We cross rivulets and cricket grounds.
Huge groups of kids get in trouble.
We rest on a bridge.
We wait for a crocodile to pass before we cross the river.

I hate how everyone thinks poems
are about sex.
They're about supper.
Oh man, my grandfather exclaimed,
I stuffed myself like a hog.
They had every kind of food you could think of,
and the quality was really good.
That is the heart of my greatest poem.
Fine quality ingredients.
But the greatest work of art would be
to drive everywhere without maps.

THE DARKNESS NEEDS A LITTLE SHOVE

*

That forest is dying
can you feel it
coming from the tops of the trees?
Keep smiling as you pass
through the lower forest of nettles

*

Beneath the rain I heard
the running legs of harder rain coming
and then I slept & dreamed of kissing her
Even with my eyes closed, the flash
of her teeth

*

A hot pan of mushrooms in the woods
white smoke & no breeze
All day airplanes mobilize the sky

*

Walking through the night forest
with just a little light
in your hand
Everything leans on you

*

A man drives away from a gas station
still pumping gas
early enough on a summer morning it's cold

*

Coming upon a wooden cross
staked in the woods at night
I turn off the flashlight
the woods begin
to eat me

*

Blue spiders
moisture on the walls
a small space
made massive
without her

*

Sadly there is something in my body
which has turned back from the hike
though my body continues on
Next year I must change
into a tree

*

Talk of politics reaches up the ridge
to the rocky outcropping
But it is very small, it fades
out. The trees don't listen

*

A snake sleeping in the sun
we come home
we get ripped
Two swallowtail butterflies
drift into love

*

Alright bugs
you don't like me
& I don't like you
but hush now, hush
everything is sleeping

*

A child wakes up laughing
it is going to rain
dark sound of a saw

*

Again I have gotten myself too involved
with the passing or holding steady of the clouds
A lawnmower suddenly cuts off—
the silence shocks black birds into the air

*

My terrible neighbor screeches outside
She disappears, the night is beautiful
it is June
I am forbidden to pass
beyond the window

*

In the busy days coming remember
to write a poem on a leaf
to write a poem in the sky

*

On the day of national mourning
I'm wearing my brightest shirt & drinking
a bird turns to me & says
"you are going to die"

*

Unwrap the first day of summer
windchimes before the storm
planes about to drop their bombs
I am full of strawberries

*

Go away, miss her
drive over a silver & blue river
go home
Breathe, breathe
the darkness needs a little shove

STATISTICS OF DEADLY QUARRELS

I read STATISTICS
OF DEADLY QUARRELS. It helped
take my mind off all the wars
plotting them on X and Y
axes. I stretched out on my
beaten-in bed and my head
disappeared in the middle
of my old yellow pillow.
Dark storm clouds then horrible
sunshine outside. Nothing dried.
Pinging outside from a drill
on stone or concrete. Police
throughout the city wearing
new pants, with cargo pockets
because of the increased threat
it was important to stress.
Sleep. Sleep. I will drift into a place
overhung with stars.
Breakfast. The breath
of the August streets, garbage
confounding pedestrians
in the morning. Sleep through this
into a memory of being too shy

to interrupt and say
something: what would I have said?
Dream baffling as the morning.
There is a small
child there. He wants me to read
to him for 30 minutes.
Rocking chair
beside a dirty window
years of yellow paint around the sill.
A few leaves dapple the light
and the smell of frying french
fries is glorious and I
see vermilion in a window box
and my grandmother
tending to her pink flowers.
I'm still sleeping. She can't move
her left side now, she sent me
a letter to my sister
by mistake.
I read some Polish poems
and noticed many of the
poets attended a school
called the Jagiellonian

Institute. My head was buried
my wife pulled sheets
over us at 3 A.M.
Something in my head wanted
sunrise
The third person who passed me
on the street was wearing a
shirt from Jagiellonian Institute
smeared by the horrible sunshine.
I feel sorry for my shirts.
I never wear them.
Carbon and hydrogen atoms have
deadly quarrels. Stars keep spewing
because the laws of physics
cannot be broken,
only ignored. Our house
a terrible current
manifestation of the cosmos
leaks love. Our last
place was comfortably set
above a basement,
haunted by a yellow arm
with fur and enormous claws.

A dark cloud has come
to sit down on us.
The leaves turn silver,
they tremble, they love the world.
I didn't really eat lunch.
Above me one of my shirts
is waving. Goodbye.
I will see you outside in
a little heap on the street.
A birthday party for Jack
The smell of chicken frying.
Glorious.
I inhale it and feel it
at the very tip of my spine.
This glorious energy
is what the ancients called the
Kundalini, the snake that
unfurls from the base of your
spine. Last weekend
while the others were sleeping
I felt this
explosion of good feelings
coming from the base of my

skull. A conveyor,
energy traveling in an ellipse.
The smell of the fried chicken.
Sunlight.
I'm hiding on my belly beneath green
fan blades and an unhealthy
tree. Now a heightened alert
strips away the clouds.
The graph can easily
be ignored. The Earth rotates,
clocks rotate.
My wife washed my hair last night.
I couldn't sleep. I twisted
in the blue and white striped sheet.
High above jet engines growled
in gray jet planes bristling with
50 calibre machine guns.
I must remember never
to quarrel, I'm too poor.
I'm made of stars, we all are, we are
made of hydrogen.
The fan stirs up the droplets.
A black cat sucks on his tail

beside me in bed. Whatever
effect these pills are going
to have it will be as real as waking up,
atoms, atoms, everything is real.
It's 9 o'clock P.M.
Caramelized onions smell more strongly here
at the end of the hallway,
like the apartment on 10th
street, when I was cooking I
used to walk to the living
room to check on the progress.
The door upstairs
to the roof was always open,
the house breathed, the house
was open to the yellow
stars, someone could probably
explain it better than me:
the horrible feeling in
the basement seemed to escape.
Every couple in the top
apartment broke up,
fighting each other over
the fire escape and into

our place. We were at the movies.
Now I have a spreading rash
from a tick that bit my ass
in the woods, on a wooded
path to Oyster Pond.
I only went there because
a sign said it was one of
Montauk's undiscovered jewels.
The trail opened out
to a clearing, the sunshine
was like a large wet sheet hung
overhead, I thought I could
smell it but what do I know?
Sleep, sleep, soon
the deadly quarrel will be
behind us.
When we wake up
the implications are terrifying.
Warnings from 3 or 4 years ago
threaten commerce. The partly
employed, those like me, don't care.
Diurnal ruptures tremble
on the surface of the sun.

The Earth is dead, not one breath
of wind. The city turns on
tiny fountains in the parks.
Sunspots are rippling outward,
8 minutes later they hit
us. I tell the boy "the sun
is a cruel master." He squirms.
The Geats besieged the Danes,
their deadly quarrel drifts away, it sinks
back down on us.
The sickness has me boxed in,
my legs are drawn up inside
my head, quiet, dark.
Rolling storms on the surface
of the sun, their enormous
pink and green blossoms settle
on our faces. There are cops
everywhere today.
It is also raining white
petals, delicately tinged
with brown, with dead brown edges.
Terror takes me apart and leaves me sleepless.
I have to lie with my sleeping

wife beside me,
she is walking beside the Allegheny River
in her sleep.
She will sit up in bed and cry
just a little
terror. Then she'll drink water.
The doctor has prescribed rain.
A stranger on the street says
the sun is about to die,
she claps me on the back, now
go, she says, about your day
knowing tomorrow you will
cast no shadow. A cheeseburger
lights up in my memory.
The red clock keeps ticking
minutes, but are they really
passing? Nothing is changing,
it is the same clock my wife
slept with, slept with it in bed
before I knew her. Then we
met, and the truly blessed, when they
draw the Sword of Resentment,
are showered in blossoms.

When the room is fully dark
I will go to the corner
store to buy a few cold beers.
No one will touch me. I won't
say a word. The strategy
of nuclear deterrence
is working admirably.
On the surface of Venus
perpetually shrouded
in clouds, the part of me I
keep most secret is soaking
in a porcelain bathtub.
And I look at myself there
in the hot water and see
that I am a planet-wide
catastrophe. I sleep
imperfectly, I'm covered
by my wife, she thinks I said
something hurtful on purpose,
she rolls away, down a hill.
Like Johannes Kepler I am going to
digress until I have glimpsed
the co-eternal glory.

A key turns in the deadbolt,
it's my wife, she's home from work.
A new song is sung unto
her green dress and her long legs.
One pleasant summer
afternoon she stooped
to examine the shell
of a bivalve at Montauk
where a red flag flew over
the beach and our intentions.
Her face is more beautiful
than all the physical laws,
and I sat down in the sand
where her elegance began
and the waves and the blue sky
won't end. And I did not even
despair of my salvation.

If a man could pass through Paradise in a Dream, & have a flower presented to him as a pledge that his Soul had really been there, & found that flower in his hand when he awoke—Aye! and what then?

SAMUEL TAYLOR COLERIDGE

ACKNOWLEDGMENTS

A section of "In a Bower of Rosemary" appeared in *The Iowa Review*. Thank you David Hamilton.

Sections of "The Ideograms" appeared in *Soft Targets* (thank you Dan Hoy); *Backwards City Review* (thank you Tom Christopher); *CutBank* (thank you Brandon Shimoda); and as an electronic chapbook in the Bear Parade series (thank you Gene Morgan and Tao Lin).

"Statistics of Deadly Quarrels" appeared at Failbetter.com. Thank you Ben Gantcher and Thom Didato.

"Poem for the East River" appeared in *Black Clock*. Thank you Arielle Greenberg.

"Poem (You called)," "Winning Isn't Everything," and "A Hawk is on Her Heart" appeared in *Make*. Thank you Joel Craig.

"Poem on the Radio" appeared in *CROWD*. Thank you Brett Fletcher Lauer and Aimee Kelley.

"Four Romantic Poets" appeared in *Twaddle*. Thank you Ryan Bird.

"Sharp" appeared in *Volt*. Thank you Gillian Conoley.

The translation of the Chuang Tzu quotation is by Martin Palmer and Elizabeth Breuilly.

Thank you Matthew Zapruder for your amazing guidance with this book. Thank you Joshua Beckman and Anthony McCann for your constant help and friendship. Thank you Susie for your unending support and love, and for help with these poems. Thank you Bert Hornback and Yunus Tuncel for the translation. Thank you Lori, Monica and Charlie for everything.

"The Ideograms" is for Seamus.

"The Darkness Needs a Little Shove" is for Han Shan.